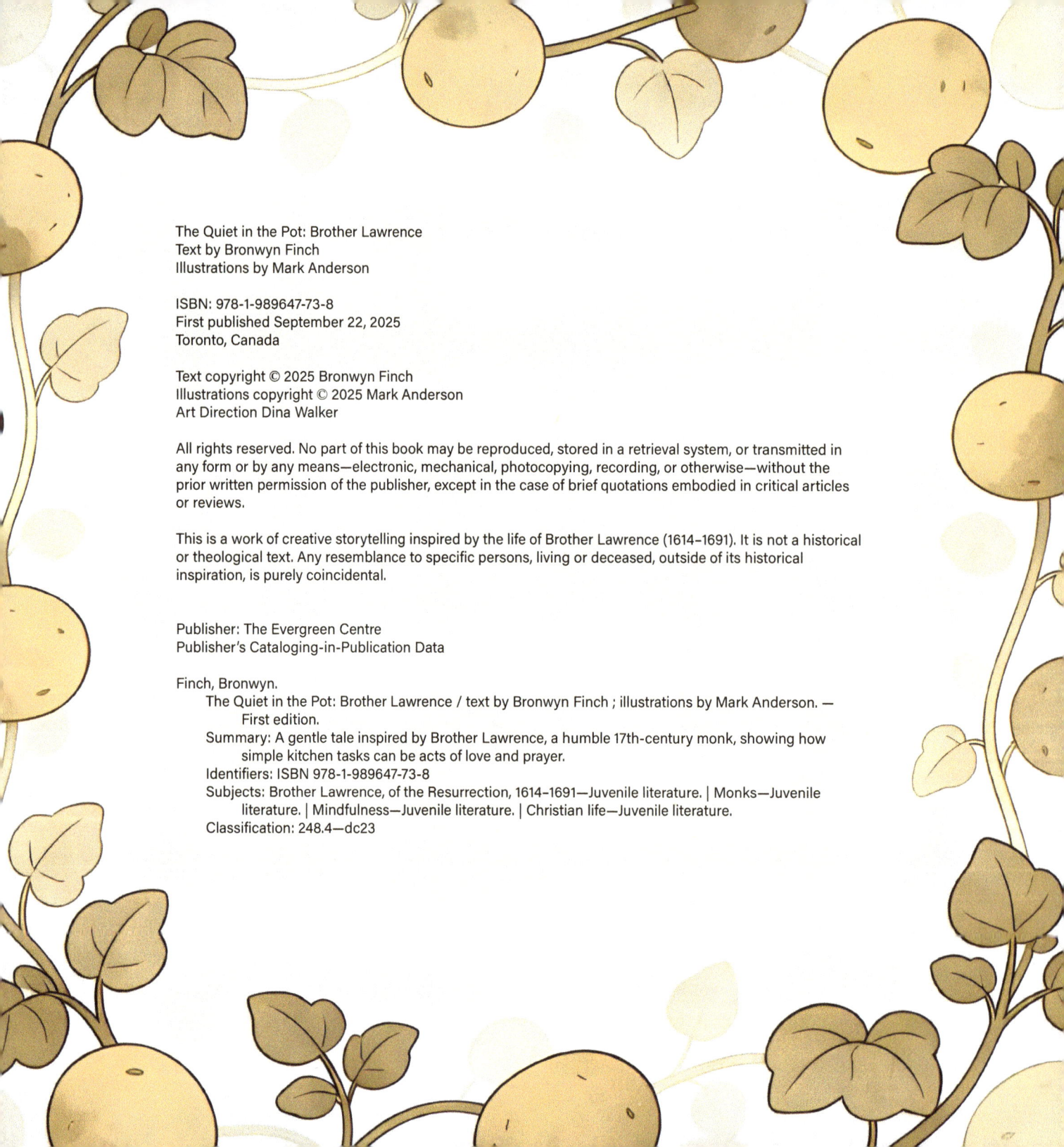

The Quiet in the Pot: Brother Lawrence
Text by Bronwyn Finch
Illustrations by Mark Anderson

ISBN: 978-1-989647-73-8
First published September 22, 2025
Toronto, Canada

Text copyright © 2025 Bronwyn Finch
Illustrations copyright © 2025 Mark Anderson
Art Direction Dina Walker

All rights reserved. No part of this book may be reproduced, stored in a retrieval system, or transmitted in any form or by any means—electronic, mechanical, photocopying, recording, or otherwise—without the prior written permission of the publisher, except in the case of brief quotations embodied in critical articles or reviews.

This is a work of creative storytelling inspired by the life of Brother Lawrence (1614–1691). It is not a historical or theological text. Any resemblance to specific persons, living or deceased, outside of its historical inspiration, is purely coincidental.

Publisher: The Evergreen Centre
Publisher's Cataloging-in-Publication Data

Finch, Bronwyn.
    The Quiet in the Pot: Brother Lawrence / text by Bronwyn Finch ; illustrations by Mark Anderson. — First edition.
    Summary: A gentle tale inspired by Brother Lawrence, a humble 17th-century monk, showing how simple kitchen tasks can be acts of love and prayer.
    Identifiers: ISBN 978-1-989647-73-8
    Subjects: Brother Lawrence, of the Resurrection, 1614–1691—Juvenile literature. | Monks—Juvenile literature. | Mindfulness—Juvenile literature. | Christian life—Juvenile literature.
    Classification: 248.4—dc23

THE QUIET IN THE POT

The Story of Brother Lawrence

by Bronwyn Finch

In a town of wind and stone,
a boy named Nicolas watched with quiet eyes.
The church bells rang. The market hummed.
But a hush called to him—
a stillness beneath the noise.
In the quiet, he felt God.

He grew tall like sunflowers,
silent as snowfall.
When war came, he marched,
but swords and shouting did not
fit his heart.
He longed for peace in small things.

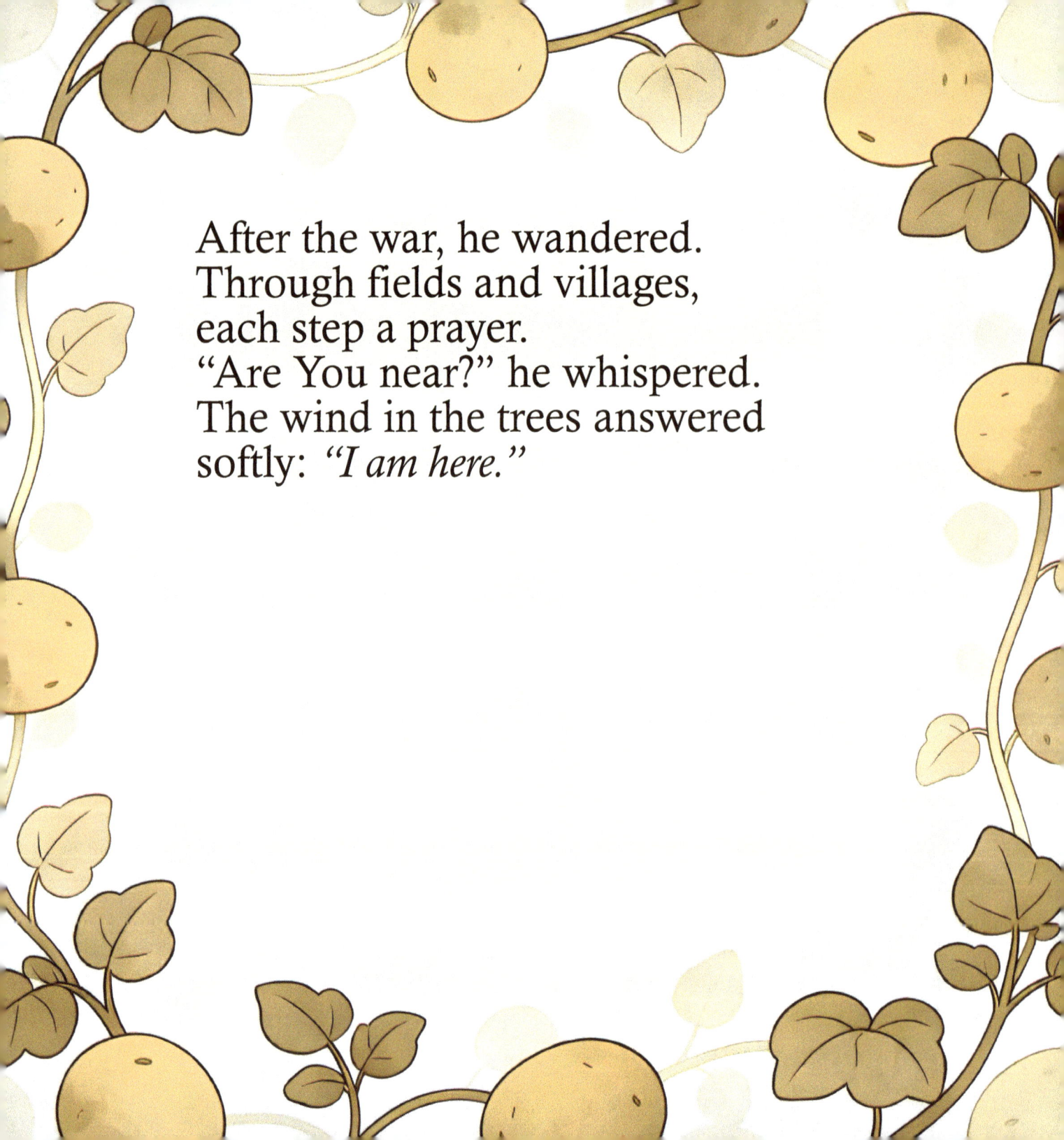

After the war, he wandered.
Through fields and villages,
each step a prayer.
"Are You near?" he whispered.
The wind in the trees answered
softly: *"I am here."*

His feet led him to a monastery.
Stone walls. Wooden doors.
A place for prayer. A place for work.
They gave him a robe,
a bed,
and a pile of potatoes.

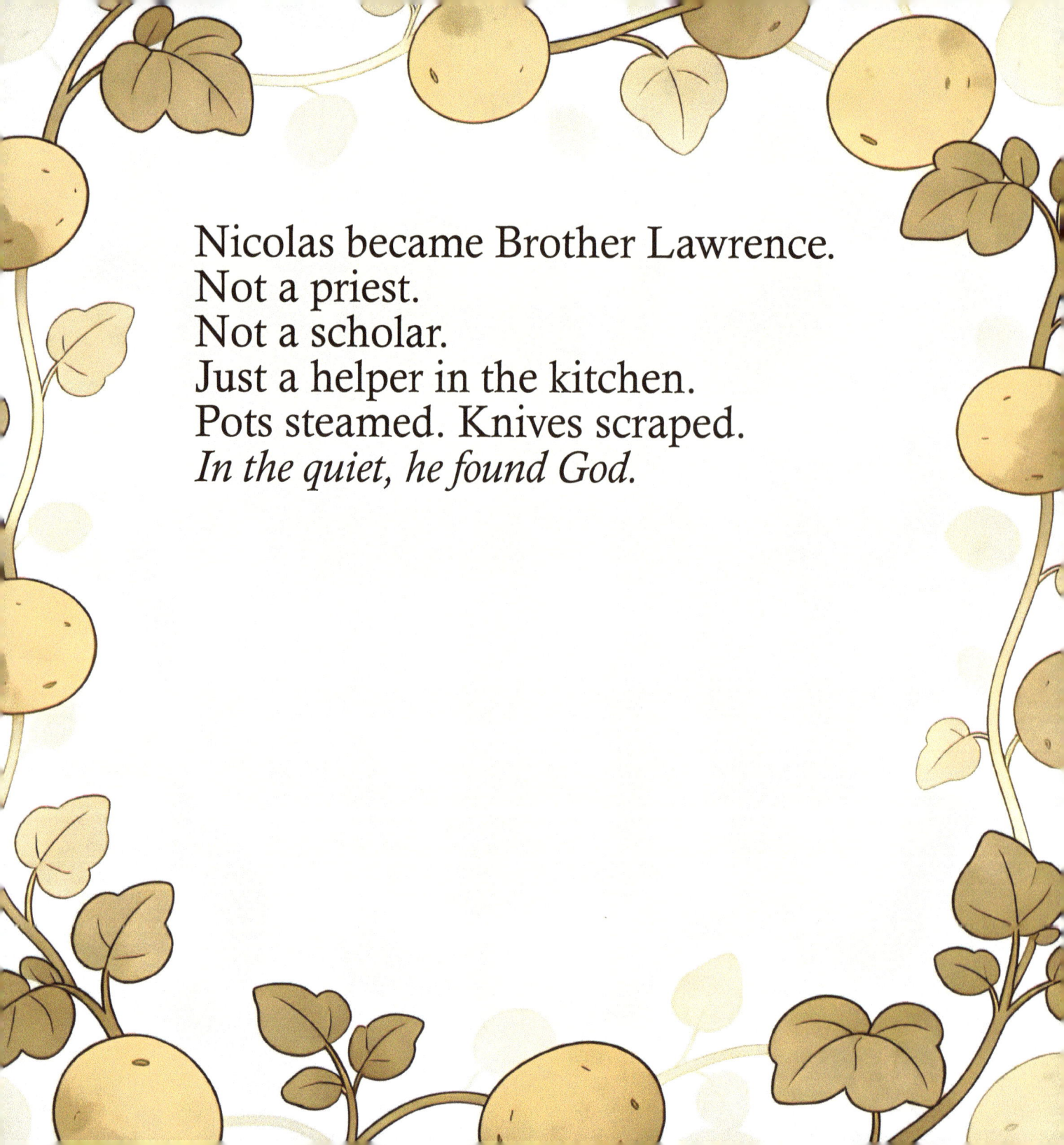

Nicolas became Brother Lawrence.
Not a priest.
Not a scholar.
Just a helper in the kitchen.
Pots steamed. Knives scraped.
In the quiet, he found God.

He peeled potatoes, slow and careful.
Each slice a whisper of love.
"This I do with You," he murmured to God.

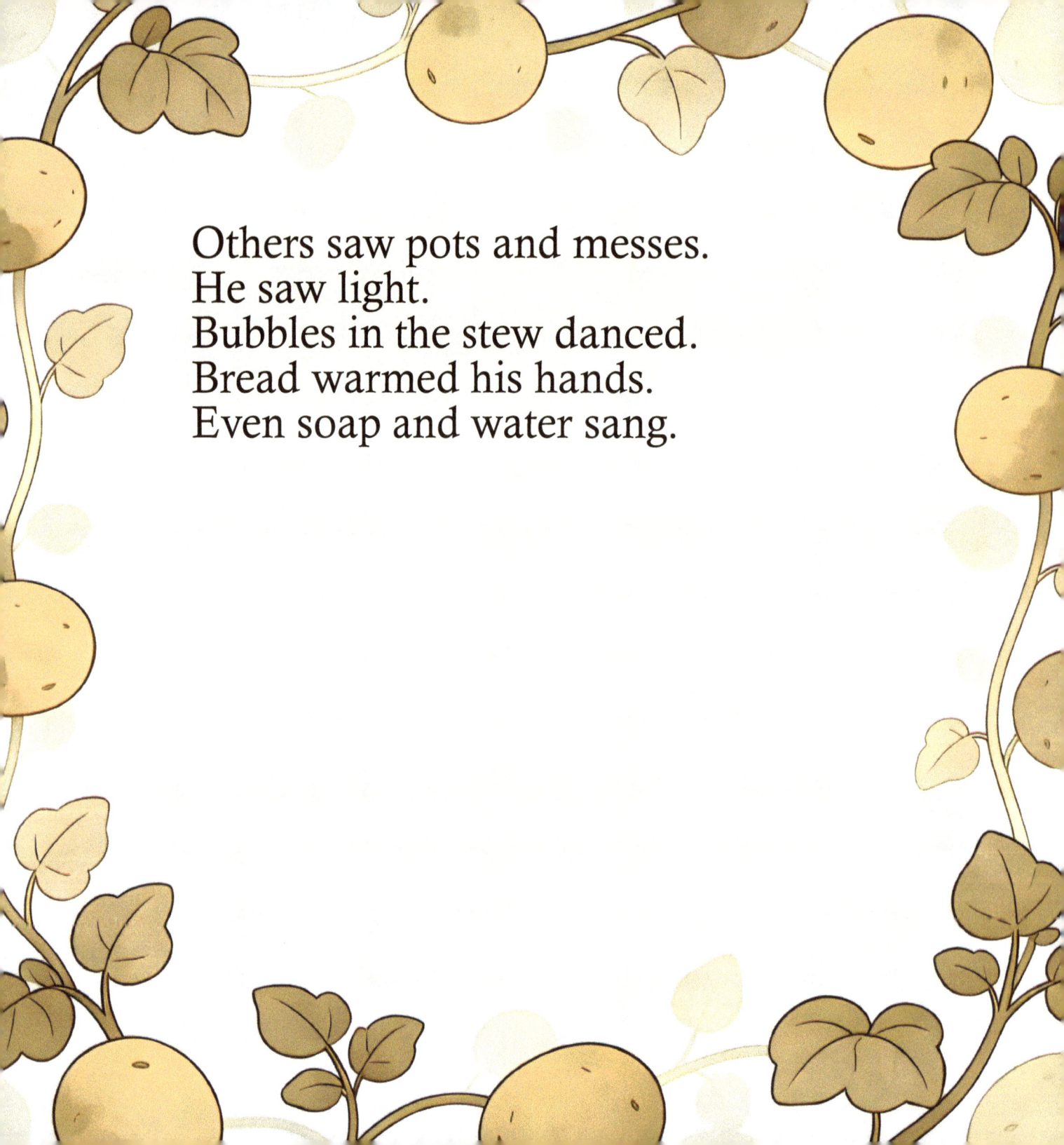

Others saw pots and messes.
He saw light.
Bubbles in the stew danced.
Bread warmed his hands.
Even soap and water sang.

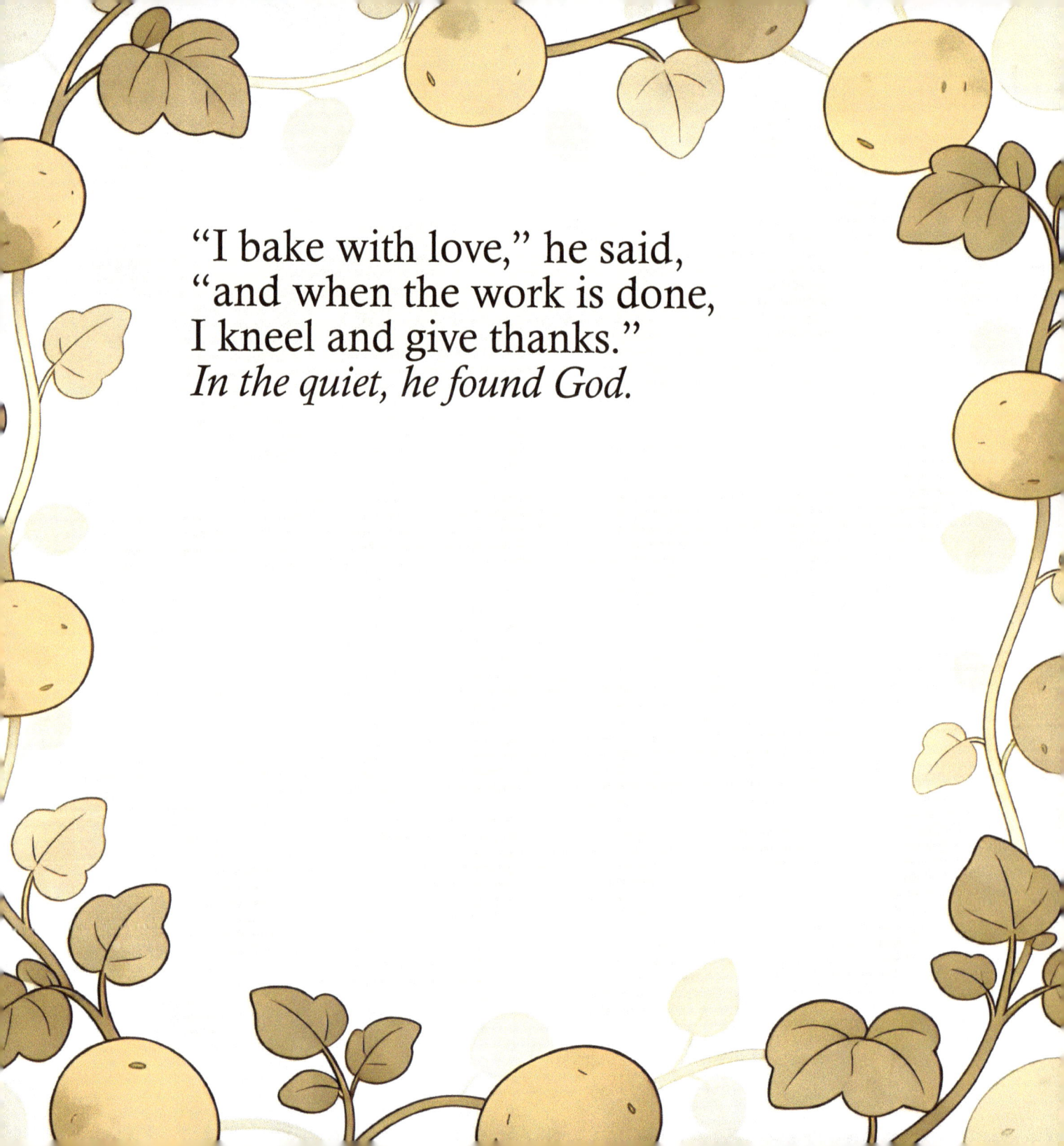

"I bake with love," he said,
"and when the work is done,
I kneel and give thanks."
In the quiet, he found God.

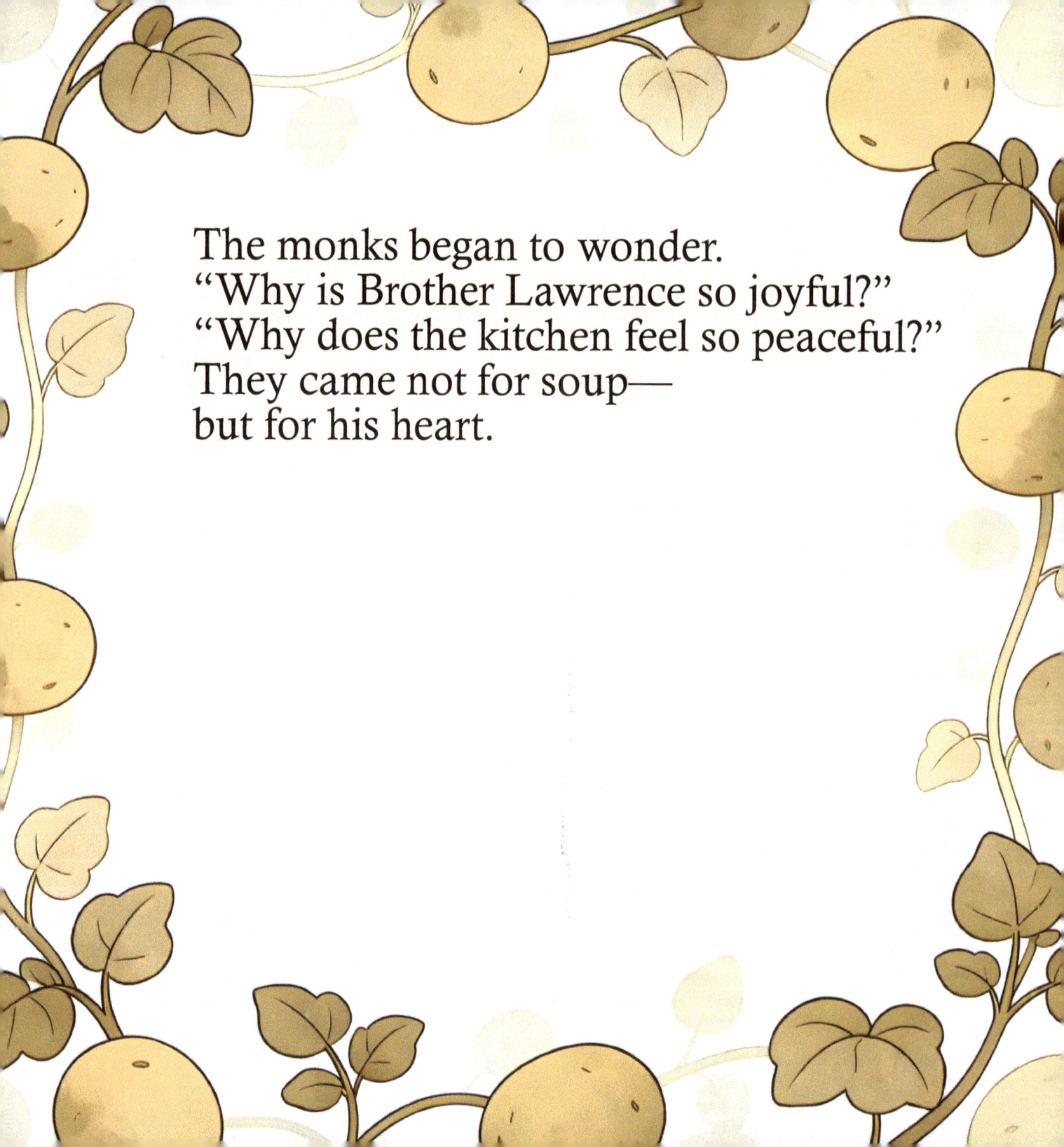

The monks began to wonder.
"Why is Brother Lawrence so joyful?"
"Why does the kitchen feel so peaceful?"
They came not for soup—
but for his heart.

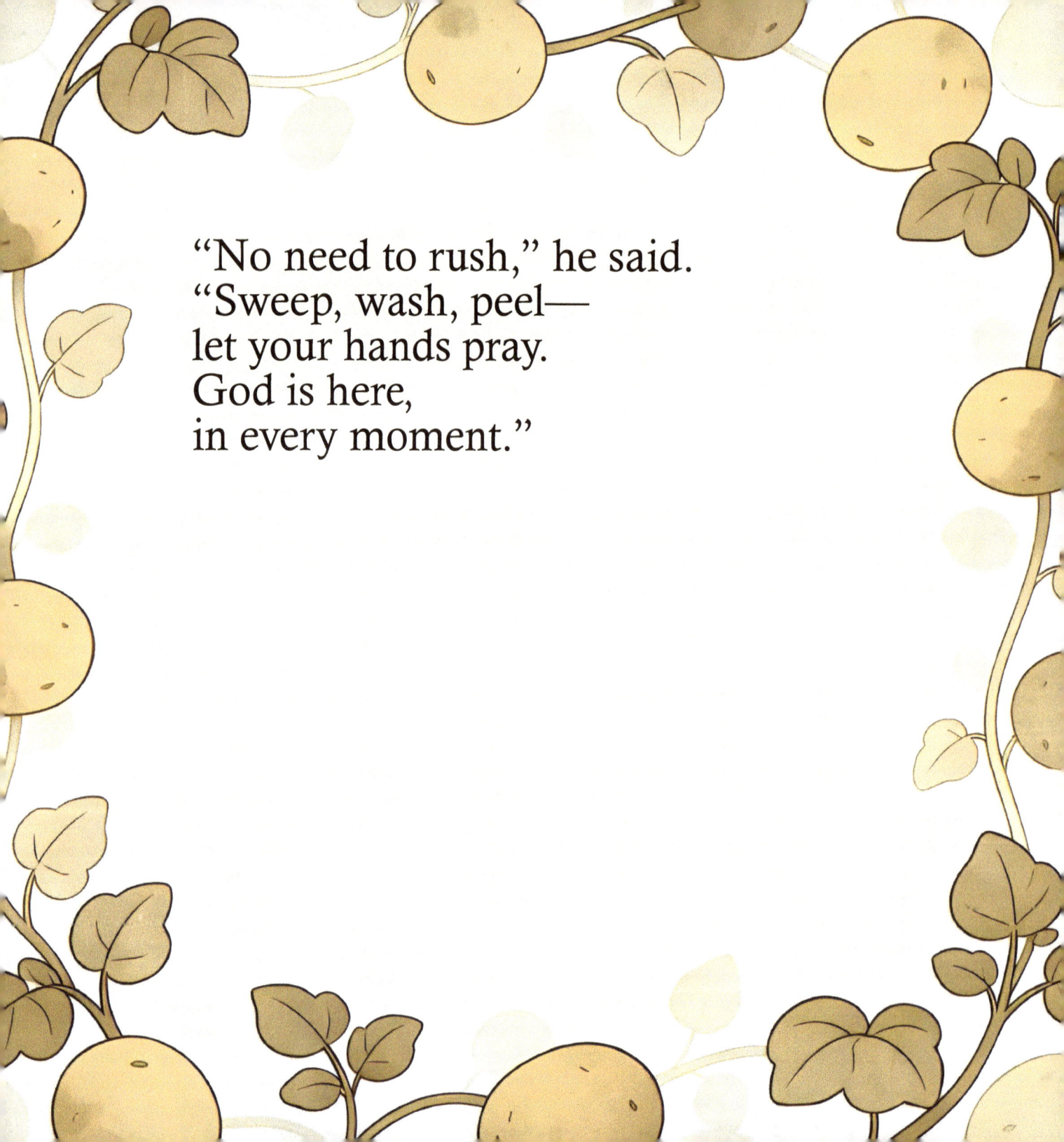

"No need to rush," he said.
"Sweep, wash, peel—
let your hands pray.
God is here,
in every moment."

He wrote no books.
But his words, simple and true,
spread like seeds.
People heard and felt hope:
God was near—
in pots, in pans, in every breath.

As Brother Lawrence grew old,
his steps slowed,
but his joy never faded.
He stirred with care.
He smiled with his whole heart.

When he was gone,
the kitchen felt still.
But only for a moment.
The quiet remained—
like a heartbeat in the world.

And today,
if you peel a potato slowly,
or stir a soup with love,
or sweep in silence—
you might feel it too.

A warmth.
A whisper.
A presence.

"I am here," you say.
"And You are too."
In the quiet, you find God
— just like Brother Lawrence.

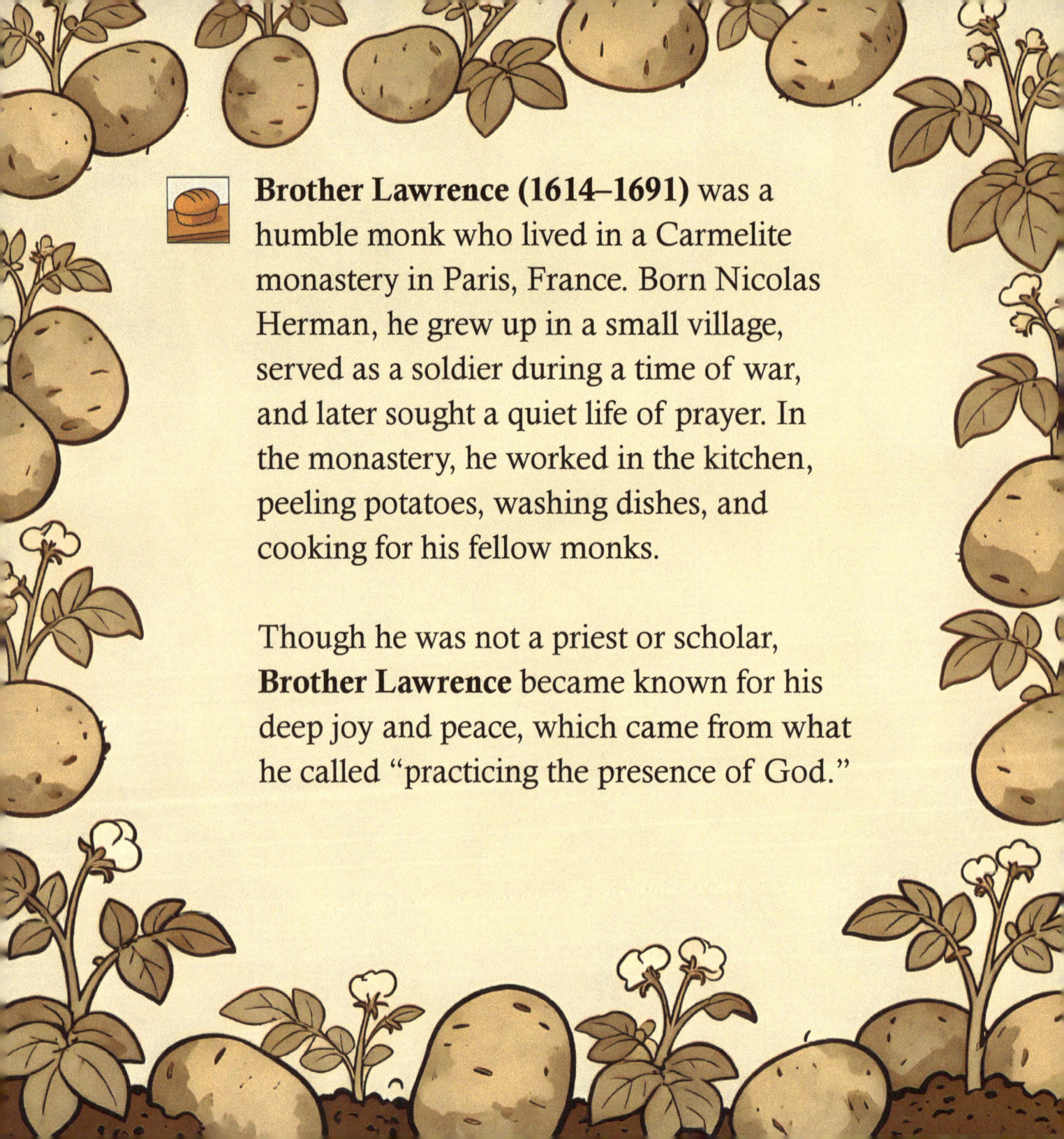

Brother Lawrence (1614–1691) was a humble monk who lived in a Carmelite monastery in Paris, France. Born Nicolas Herman, he grew up in a small village, served as a soldier during a time of war, and later sought a quiet life of prayer. In the monastery, he worked in the kitchen, peeling potatoes, washing dishes, and cooking for his fellow monks.

Though he was not a priest or scholar, **Brother Lawrence** became known for his deep joy and peace, which came from what he called "practicing the presence of God."

For **Brother Lawrence**, every task—no matter how small—was a chance to connect with God. Whether stirring a pot or sweeping the floor, he believed that ordinary moments could be filled with love and prayer. His simple wisdom, shared through conversations and a few letters, inspired people far beyond his monastery.

His teachings were later collected in a book called **The Practice of the Presence of God**, which continues to guide those seeking mindfulness and faith in daily life.

Like him, we can discover that the quiet moments—whether cooking, cleaning, or simply breathing—are opportunities to feel a deeper connection to something greater.

🍞 Kitchen Devotionals: Practicing Presence in the Ordinary

Practicing Presence in the Kitchen
The kitchen is a place of transformation—where raw things become nourishing, where hands work quietly, and where time itself is folded into the rhythm of preparation.

If this book has invited you to notice the sacred in the ordinary, then let these simple tasks become small liturgies. Peeling, stirring, sweeping, waiting: each one holds a whisper of grace. These reflections are not instructions, but invitations—to slow down, to pay attention, and to let your work become prayer.

🥄 Using Carrot Greens
Nothing is wasted.
Even what's often discarded can nourish.
God, show me the value in what I overlook.

🥄 Stirring Soup
Blend what is separate.
Each ingredient contributes. Together, they become something new.
God, stir peace into my day.

🥄 Sweeping Crumbs
Even the smallest things matter.
Tiny remnants, brushed away with care.
God, help me tend to the overlooked.

🥄 Setting the Table
Prepare space for joy.
A place for each person. A moment to pause.
God, let my hospitality be holy.

🥄 Boiling Water
Transformation takes time.
Stillness becomes movement. Cold becomes heat.
God, teach me to wait with hope.

🥄 Cracking Eggs
Brokenness can nourish.
The shell breaks. Life begins.
God, use even my broken places for good.

🥄 Composting Scraps
Leftovers help new things grow.
What we don't need goes back to the earth.
God, make the world fresh and full again.

🥄 Drying Dishes
Finish with care.
The final step, quiet and gentle.
God, help me complete what I begin.

🥄 Measuring Flour
God is in the details.
Too much, too little—balance matters.
God, help me live with intention.

🥄 Kneading Dough

Mix and rise in time.
Hands press and fold. The dough rests, then grows.
God, shape me slowly. Let me rise in Your time.

🥄 Cooling Bread

Even warmth needs pause.
Fresh from the oven, it waits.
God, teach me to rest before I serve.

🍞 Closing Blessing

May your kitchen be a sanctuary.
May your hands be gentle, your heart
    attentive, and your work a prayer.
God is here—in the peeling, the stirring,
    the sweeping, the waiting.

www.ingramcontent.com/pod-product-compliance
Lightning Source LLC
Chambersburg PA
CBHW061356010526
44107CB00012B/952